My Engineering Library

Design and Build It to Go

Nikole Brooks Bethea

Rourke Educational Media
A Division of Carson Dellosa Education

ROURKE'S
SCHOOL to HOME
CONNECTIONS

BEFORE AND DURING READING ACTIVITIES

Before Reading: *Building Background Knowledge and Vocabulary*

Building background knowledge can help children process new information and build upon what they already know. Before reading a book, it is important to tap into what children already know about the topic. This will help them develop their vocabulary and increase their reading comprehension.

Questions and Activities to Build Background Knowledge:

1. Look at the front cover of the book and read the title. What do you think this book will be about?
2. What do you already know about this topic?
3. Take a book walk and skim the pages. Look at the table of contents, photographs, captions, and bold words. Did these text features give you any information or predictions about what you will read in this book?

Vocabulary: *Vocabulary Is Key to Reading Comprehension*

Use the following directions to prompt a conversation about each word.

- Read the vocabulary words.
- What comes to mind when you see each word?
- What do you think each word means?

Vocabulary Words:
- *engines*
- *gravity*
- *lift*
- *pollution*

During Reading: *Reading for Meaning and Understanding*

To achieve deep comprehension of a book, children are encouraged to use close reading strategies. During reading, it is important to have children stop and make connections. These connections result in deeper analysis and understanding of a book.

Close Reading a Text

During reading, have children stop and talk about the following:

- Any confusing parts
- Any unknown words
- Text to text, text to self, text to world connections
- The main idea in each chapter or heading

Encourage children to use context clues to determine the meaning of any unknown words. These strategies will help children learn to analyze the text more thoroughly as they read.

When you are finished reading this book, turn to the last page for an **After Reading Activity**.

Table of Contents

The Problem of Air

Engineers design ways for us to go all over the place!

What do engineers have to think about to help us get from place to place?

Engineers design cars. As cars move, air pushes against them. This slows them down.

Engineers make **engines** that push vehicles forward. The force of the push must be greater than the force of the air.

Engineers also shape cars so that air flows around them. Fast cars are curved and smooth. Box-shaped cars are slower.

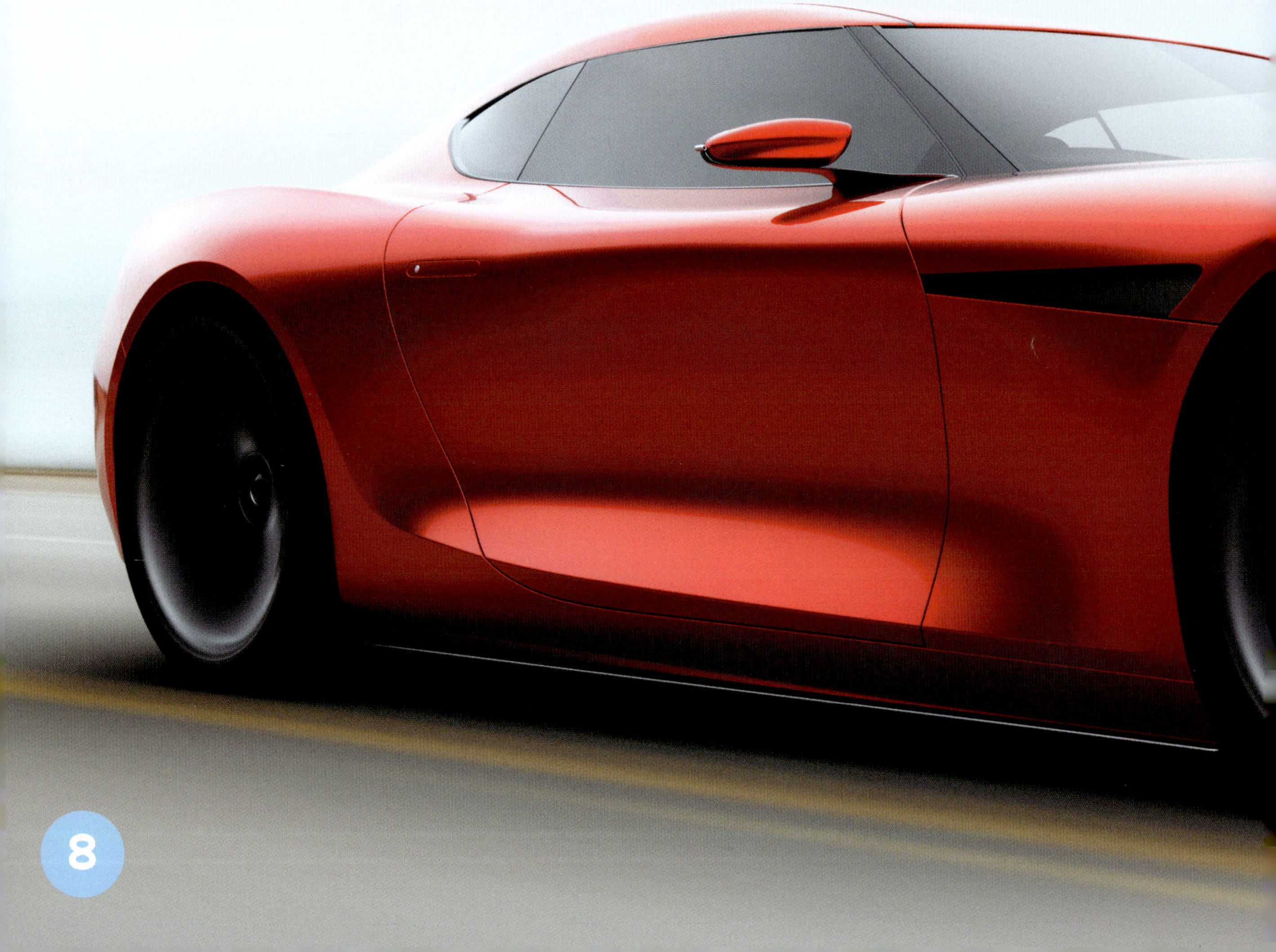

slower vehicle
faster vehicle

SPACEX

The Problem of Gravity

Gravity is the force that pulls things toward Earth. Gravity keeps heavy rockets close to the Earth.

How do engineers help get rockets off the ground?

They design rocket engines. The engines burn fuel. Engines push the rocket up. The push becomes greater than the force of gravity. The rocket blasts off!

Forces on a rocket

What about airplanes? How do engineers make them fly?

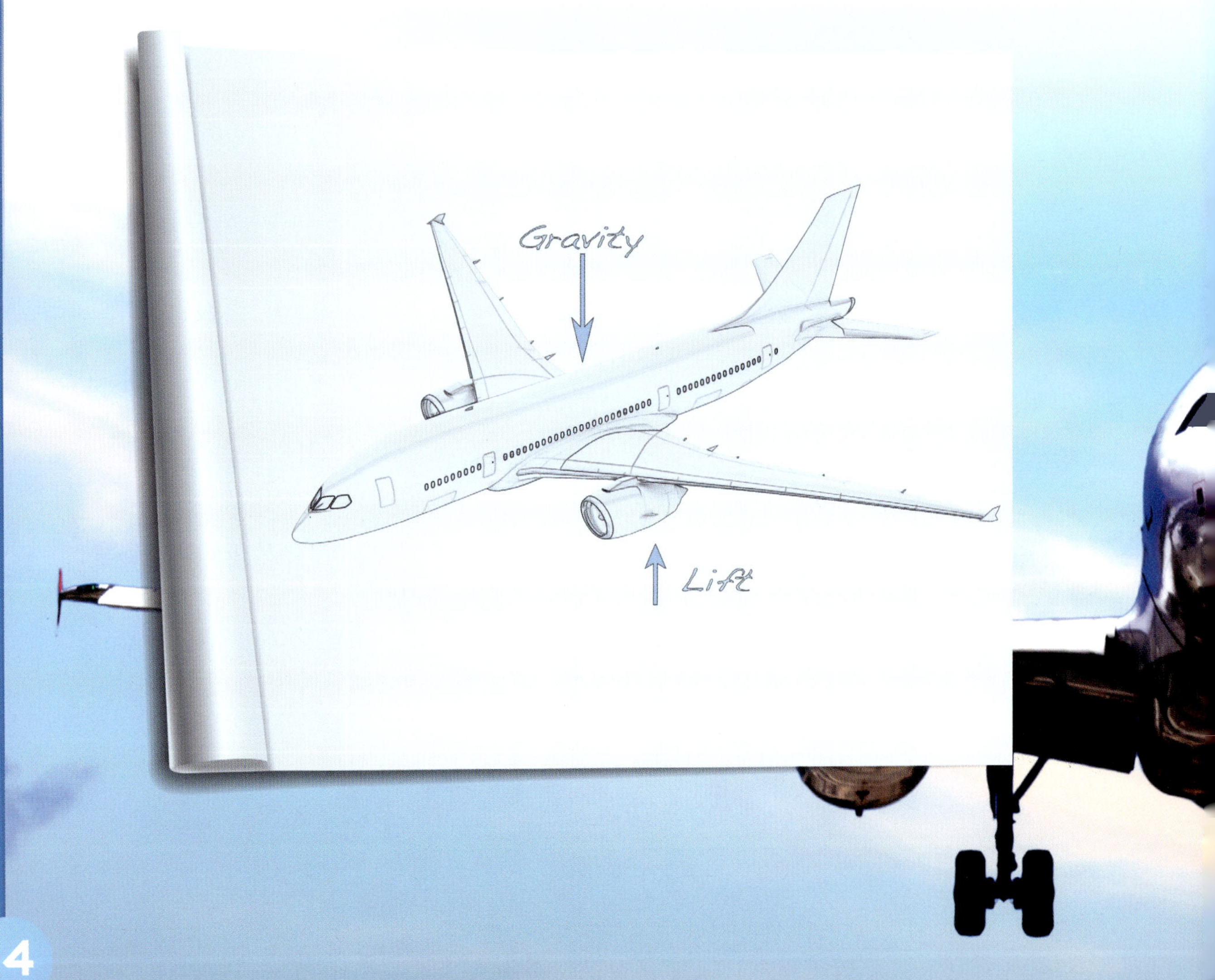

They design airplane wings with special shapes. Air flows under the wings. This makes **lift**. The upward force of lift works against the force of gravity. The plane flies!

The Problem of Pollution

Many machines that go make **pollution** when they burn fuel. How do engineers help make less pollution?

They make special trains. Maglev trains don't burn fuel. They don't make pollution. They use the force of magnets to move.

也能成为水库
SMT

Have you ever played with a pair of magnets? Touching two sides one direction makes magnets stick together. If you flip one magnet over, forces push the two apart.

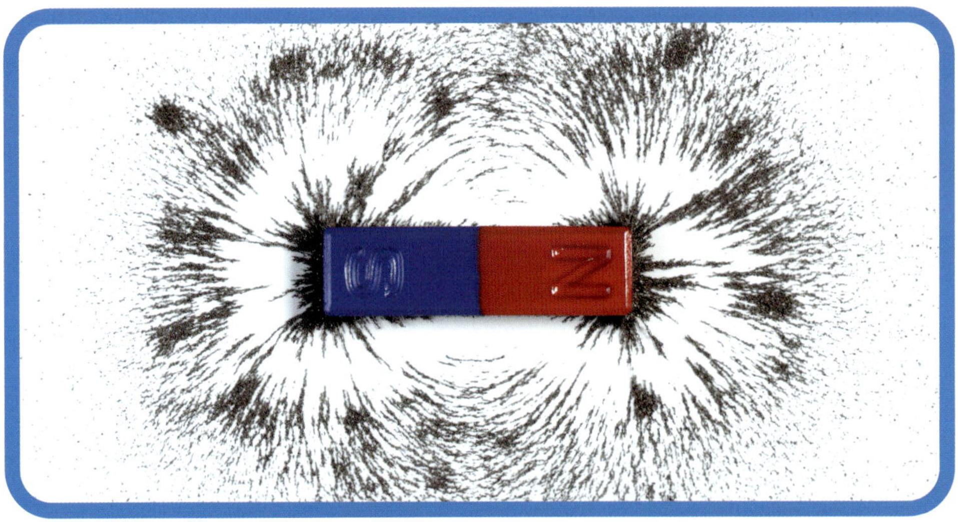

This is how maglev trains work! Magnets coming together pull the train forward. Magnets pushing apart make the train push up and float over the track.

What ways to go will engineers design next?

Photo Glossary

engines (EN-jins): Machines that make something move by using an energy source.

gravity (GRAV-i-tee): The force that pulls things toward the center of the Earth.

lift (lift): An upward force that acts on an airplane wing.

pollution (puh-LOO-shuhn): Harmful substances or waste released into the environment.

Engineering Design Activity

What design will you use for a boat?

Supplies

aluminum foil
small tub, dishpan, or bucket half-filled with water
100 pennies

Directions

Boats float because a buoyant force pushes up on them from the water below. Design a boat that will hold the most cargo without sinking. Form the aluminum foil into a shape that you think will float and support the most weight. Place the boat in the water. Does it float? Begin loading it with one penny at a time. Count how many pennies you can add until it sinks.

Index

About the Author

In addition to writing children's science books, Nikole Brooks Bethea is a professional engineer. Her designs have included tall water tanks, systems to treat drinking water and wastewater, and underground water and wastewater utilities. She lives in the Florida Panhandle with her husband and four sons.

After Reading Activity

Make a list of ways you have traveled or wish to travel. Now, think about how engineers designed each vehicle. Write one force that makes each vehicle go. Write one force that slows each vehicle down.

Library of Congress PCN Data

Design and Build It to Go / Nikole Brooks Bethea
(My Engineering Library)
ISBN (hard cover)(alk. paper) 978-1-73163-850-2
ISBN (soft cover) 978-1-73163-927-1
ISBN (e-Book) 978-1-73164-004-8
ISBN (e-Pub) 978-1-73164-081-9
Library of Congress Control Number: 2020930245

Rourke Educational Media
Printed in the United States of America
06-020251937

www.rourkeeducationalmedia.com

Edited by: Hailey Scragg
Cover and interior design by: Rhea Magaro-Wallace
Photo Credits: Cover logo: frog ©Eric Phol, test tube ©Sergey Lazarev, cover tab art ©siridhata, cover photo ©Arana; Page 5: ©Marilyn Nieves; Page 6: ©Rawpixel; Pages 7, 22: ©Stefan Schulze; Pages 8, 9: ©Arand, Page 9: ©vitpho; Page 10: ©NASA ; Page 13: ©NASA; Pages 13, 22: ©jamesbenet; Pages 14, 15: ©gece33; Page 14, 22: ©Robert Churchill Pages 17, 22: ©Greg Kelton; Pages 18, 19:©holgs; Page 20: ©Wittayayut; Page 21: ©kirza